A Gallery of Mothers and Their Children

With text by MARIAN KING

J. B. LIPPINCOTT COMPANY PHILADELPHIA · NEW YORK

*For my mother
and for all mothers*

AUTHOR'S NOTE

I WISH to express my appreciation for the valuable cooperation rendered me by the directors and staffs of the galleries, museums and libraries whose pictures are reproduced by special permission in this volume. I also wish to thank the galleries and museums, whose works I was unable to use, for their generous support.

I am extremely grateful for the splendid assistance and cooperation of the following at the Library of Congress: Colonel Willard Webb and Mr. Gordon Patterson, Stack and Reader Division; Mr. Legare Obear, Chief of the Loan Division; Mr. Thomas Shaw, Head of the Public Reference Section; Miss Alice Parker, Chief Assistant of the Prints and Photograph Section; Mrs. Grace Fuller and Mrs. Lucile Haseman, Bibliography and Reference Correspondence Section.

I am grateful to the following members of the staff of the Public Library, Washington, D.C.: Mr. Firman Wilson, Mr. Marchal Landgren and Miss Lois Stiles of the Art Division, and Miss Georgia Cowan, Chief of the Biography Division.

A special expression of gratitude is due the following for their constructive guidance and untiring help: the excellent and wonderfully cooperative staff of the Reference Room of the Frick Art Reference Library; Mr. Charles Coleman Sellers, author, and librarian of Dickinson College, Carlisle, Pennsylvania, and Belknap Library, Winterthur, Delaware; Mr. Richard Norris Williams II, Director of The Historical Society of Pennsylvania; Dr. Joseph C. Sloane, Professor of History of Art, Bryn Mawr College; Mr. David McKibbin of the Boston Athenaeum; and Mr. Carlton Lake of Paris, France.

Washington, D.C.   *Marian King*

CONTENTS

COUNTESS LUCIA THIENE DA PORTO WITH HER DAUGHTER PORZIA

By Paolo Veronese (1528-1588) Venetian School

Walters Art Gallery, Baltimore
Canvas 81 x 47½ inches. Painted c. 1556.

THIS portrait of the Countess Lucia Thiene da Porto and her daughter Porzia is a companion to Veronese's painting of her husband, the Count Giuseppe da Porto, and their son Adriano, which is in Florence. The da Portos were both natives of Vicenza.

Stately and serene, the Countess stands on a brown-gray, tiled floor against a gray-brown background. Her dark brown hair is parted in the center and combed off her ears. Tight ringlets border her high broad forehead and a jeweled snood catches her hair at the back. Her large brown eyes, under delicately curved brows in a round fair face, have a pensive look. The white and gold yoke of her orange-red velvet dress ends in a stand-up collar. Gold lace softens the lines of her bodice. Her great coat of a rich rose-red material, trimmed with gold braid, is lined with a light fur interspersed with black tails. Over her right arm is a curious fur piece, with the head of the animal wrought in metal. It is fastened to the pendant of her gold enamel girdle. Young Porzia is a miniature, in coloring and features, of her mother. Her reddish-brown hair and snood are worn in the same manner as the countess'. The daughter wears a long brown velvet dress with a gold fabric on the sleeves and at the hem. White lace edges the neckline and cuffs. Around her neck is a double strand of amber beads, and a chain of gold girdles her waist.

Born in Verona in 1528, Paolo Caliari became known as Veronese. He first studied under his father, a sculptor. Later he turned to painting and entered the studio of Antonio Badile. When Veronese went to Venice between 1553 and 1554, he was already an accomplished artist with a number of commissions behind him. There he came in contact with Titian and Tintoretto. Among Veronese's first commissions after settling in Venice were the decorations for the church of San Sebastiano which brought him immediate acclaim. Other commissions followed rapidly. One of the most important was the re-decorating of the Doge's Palace. Veronese was a prolific painter. His works included many Biblical, mythological and allegorical subjects, and portraits. Scenes of great pageantry and feasts fascinated him. Veronese died in Venice on April 19, 1588. He was buried in the church of San Sebastiano, which had been decorated mainly by his hand.

A Young Woman and Her Little Boy

By Agnolo Bronzino (1503-1572) Florentine School

Widener Collection, National Gallery of Art, Washington, D.C.
Panel 39¾₆ x 29⅞ inches. Painted c. 1540.

THE name of this young mother, with her son, is unknown, but her family was undoubtedly a notable one. She is dressed in a gown of rose-red brocade, with a yoke of finely tucked brownish transparent material, and wears a gold chain over her shoulders. Her jeweled girdle is made of costly metals. Blue enamel and gold pendant earrings, set with pearls, match the necklace about her throat. A pearl fastens the opening of her dress. Her dress has elaborate sleeves, puffed at the top and slit in several places to show a rich lining of red and gold. In her left hand she holds brown leather gloves. Her chestnut-brown hair, finely braided at the line of her forehead, and a fitted turban, heavily embroidered in gold, form a framework for her oval face. The beautiful line of the eyebrows over her large brown eyes, and her fair complexion, bring out the sculptural quality of her patrician beauty. The small son, whose light brown hair curls about his head and face, clasps the thumb of his mother's right hand. His delicate coloring and the expression of his face are like his mother's. A fine white ruching trims the collar and cuffs of his blue-black jacket. The artist has chosen a dark green as the perfect background for this picture.

Agnolo Bronzino (Agnolo di Cosimo di Mariano) was born about 1503 in Monticelli, near Florence. After two years of study with an unknown painter, he entered the studio of Raffaelino del Garbo. Later he became the favorite pupil of Jacopo Carrucci, known as Pontormo, who trusted Bronzino to assist him with some of his most important commissions. He completed the decorations of the Chapel of San Lorenzo at Florence after Pontormo's death. Bronzino also found a friend in the painter, architect and biographer, Giorgio Vasari. In Rome in 1546 he came under the influence of Michelangelo. Adept at both oil and fresco painting, Bronzino excelled in portraiture and was the leading portrait painter of Tuscany in the sixteenth century. He painted some of the most notable personages of his day, among them Cosimo I, Grand Duke of Tuscany, and his beautiful Spanish wife.

Susanna Fourment and Her Daughter

By Sir Anthony Van Dyck (1599-1641) Flemish School

Mellon Collection, National Gallery of Art, Washington, D.C.
Canvas 68 x 46¼ inches. Painted c. 1625.

Susanna Fourment came from a middle-class family of Antwerp. Her father was a silk merchant. She had ten sisters, one of whom was Helena, the second wife of the Flemish artist and diplomat, Peter Paul Rubens.

Seated in an armchair on a columned terrace that overlooks trees and a clouded sky, Susanna Fourment is shown clasping the hands of her small daughter. Large folds of red drapery accent the white, lace-trimmed double ruff she wears about her throat. Her brownish-red hair, which she has combed off her high, wide forehead is partly covered by a jeweled cap. Expressive brown eyes and delicate features lend distinction to her small pointed oval face. The pearl earrings and choker reflect the soft tones of her flesh. Her slit black cape, with its ornamental fastenings of silver and gold chains, reveals the lace-cuffed gold bodice beneath. On her left hand Susanna wears an amethyst ring. The skirt of her daughter's frock is made of changeable orange and red silk, with narrow bands of gold above the hem. The bodice of the same material is embroidered in stripes of gold. The little girl's sleeves, set under padded wings, have lace cuffs to match her collar. A mauve scarf is draped between her skirt and her mother's. A wide ribbon is tied under her chin and over the top of her light brown hair to form a crown to the brim of her headdress.

Anthony Van Dyck, who was born in Antwerp on March 22, 1599, was only a boy of ten when he was apprenticed to the painter Hendrik van Balen. At the age of sixteen Van Dyck had become an independent painter, working at portraits and at heads of Christ and the Apostles. Three years later the Guild of St. Luke admitted him as a full member, an unusual honor for so young an artist. By that time Rubens had welcomed this young man as an assistant. During the following year Van Dyck spent some time at the court of James I of England. Following a brief visit to Flanders, the artist's cherished desire to study the great masters was realized in a visit to Italy.

In 1632 an invitation came from Charles I, now on the throne of England, to be his court painter and Van Dyck again crossed the Channel. He lived at the king's expense in apartments at Blackfriars and was given a country house in Kent. He was knighted as "Sir Anthony Vandike, principalle Paynter in ordinary to their Majesties."

PORTRAIT OF A LADY WITH HER LITTLE DAUGHTER

By Cornelis de Vos (1585-1651) Flemish School

Samuel H. Kress Collection, M. H. De Young Memorial Museum, San Francisco
Panel 43½ x 33⅞ inches. Painted 1620-1625.

ALTHOUGH Cornelis de Vos has left no record to identify this mother and child, they are probably members of a Flemish family of good standing. Before great folds of lavender-rose drapery, looped back to show a blue sky, the tall, dignified mother sits in a bright orange-red chair. She clasps the hand of her daughter. Her oval face, with its long broad nose and rather wide mouth, is dominated by large gray eyes. A jeweled snood holds her tightly drawn dark hair well above the pleated white ruff about her neck. Deep white cuffs, edged with lace, adorn her padded, puffed sleeves, which are trimmed with black ribbon to form a striped design. The skirt and bodice are of a self-patterned black fabric. Her stomacher is heavily embroidered in tones of gold and rust. The bracelets worn low on her wrists are of fine gold links, and the rings on her heavy hands are set with precious stones.The shy little girl wears a white cap on her blond hair. Her pearl-white dress, with a floral pattern in French blue, has a long skirt, slashed shoulder wings and a starched white collar bordered with lace. Her apron and matching cuffs are made of a sheer white linen trimmed with a picot edging. Her left hand rests on the long folds of the blue scarf draped over her shoulder and she playfully turns her rosy-cheeked face to show her bright gray eyes and smiling mouth.

Cornelis de Vos was born at Hulst in the province of Zeeland in the Netherlands about 1585. At fourteen he was studying in Antwerp. In 1608, de Vos became a master of the Guild of St. Luke in Antwerp and its dean from 1619 to 1620. He formed many close friendships with the leading artists of his community. His sister Margaret married the still-life and animal painter, Frans Snyders. De Vos worked with Rubens for a period, and Rubens often recommended commissions to him. De Vos's early work reflects the influence of Rubens in its florid coloring and the use of elaborate accessories. His later painting, with its more subdued color and more elegantly clad figures, shows the effect of his close association with Van Dyck. Among Van Dyck's portraits is one of de Vos and another of his sister Margaret. De Vos painted many historical and mythological scenes, but he was at his best in portraiture, especially of children. He died on May 9, 1651, at Antwerp, where he had spent most of his life.

Saskia Carrying Rumbartus Downstairs

By Rembrandt van Rijn (1606-1669) Dutch School

Pierrepont Morgan Library, New York
Pen and brown ink, and brown wash 7⅜₆ x 5¼ inches. Executed c. 1636.

RUMBARTUS, the first-born of Rembrandt's four children, was baptized on December 15, 1635. He must have been about a year old when his father made this sketch. Rembrandt's beloved wife, Saskia, one of his favorite models, is shown holding the child.

With a few lines and some washes of brown ink, expressing both strength and tenderness, Rembrandt shows the young Rumbartus clinging to his mother. The boy's legs hang limp below the strong arm that supports him. His own arm stretches across his mother's shoulder. The fretfulness in his face, sketched in half light, contrasts with the serene, almost smiling expression of the mother, whose face, in full light, is pressed close to the child's. Wearing a long gown, belted high at the waist, Saskia walks downstairs, her skirt swirling about her legs. A lace cap covers the back of her head, and a moneybag hangs from her waist.

Rembrandt van Rijn, the son of a miller, was born in Leyden. At about the age of seven he entered the Latin School in Leyden and in May of 1620 became a student at the University. When Rembrandt's father had become convinced that his son wanted to become a painter, the fifteen-year-old youth was apprenticed to Jacob Isaacsz van Swanenburgh in Leyden. Three years later Rembrandt went to Amsterdam to study under Pieter Lastman. Upon Rembrandt's return to Leyden, he set himself up as an independent painter, etching and painting the scenes and people around him. His mother was one of his favorite models. Having achieved considerable recognition in Leyden, Rembrandt moved to Amsterdam in 1631. The great success of his portrait, *Anatomy Lesson of Dr. Tulp,* a year later, not only brought Rembrandt commissions but established him as one of the leading artists in Amsterdam. His marriage to the wealthy Saskia van Uylenburgh in 1634 enabled Rembrandt to live in luxury. However, in the early 1640's, his fortunes turned. His beloved Saskia died and people began to prefer the elegant style of Van Dyck. During the last ten years of his life, up to his death in 1669 in Amsterdam, he had little money and lived in great poverty, yet Rembrandt's finest painting belongs to these difficult years.

Mrs. Ralph Winstanley Wood and Her Two Daughters

By Francis Wheatley (1747-1801) British School

Henry E. Huntington Library and Art Gallery, San Marino, California
Canvas 36 x 28 inches. Painted 1787.

This portrait is a companion to the same artist's painting of Mrs. Ralph Winstanley Wood's husband and their young son. In this scene of everyday family life, the mother's reading has been interrupted by her older daughter who offers her peaches and grapes she has gathered in a wicker basket. Turning her brown eyes and pudgy, pink, unpowdered face toward the girl, she seems to question her. A pale-gray, ruffled-lace mob cap, trimmed with a yellow satin ribbon, almost covers her pompadour of gray hair. Her full white gown is sheer enough to reveal the color of a pale-blue silk petticoat. A bow of yellow ribbon sets off the ruffles of her sleeves. Tied with a black ribbon, a locket decorates the hand in which she holds the open book. Her tall slim daughter, standing beside her, has cameo-like features and a complexion somewhat darker than her mother's. Her long dark curls hang casually over her shoulders. Ruffles edge the bodice and the bottom of the sleeves of her rather heavy white dress, and a dark green band of ribbon crosses her shoulder. She has tucked her skirt high under her arm, revealing a red shoe and a yellow silk petticoat. The younger girl to the right, has paused from her task of cutting roses. Her white frock and the delicate coloring of her skin are seen in full light against the deep shadows of the soft green pine trees that form the background of the scene. Her blond hair, cut in uneven bangs, large blue eyes, and a pointed chin give her an enchanted look. Light mauve sweet peas, deep-red poppies and pink roses add a graceful note to the foreground. In the distance, a small blue lake and the typical rolling hills of the English countryside are seen in the soft yellow light of early evening.

Francis Wheatley, son of a master tailor, was born in London. Encouraged by his father, he attended William Shipley's drawing school and was later one of the first students admitted to the Royal Academy School. He exhibited with the Society of Artists when he was eighteen. In 1779 Wheatley went to Ireland and worked in Dublin. He did not return to London until a few years later. During his early years he was successful as a portrait painter. It was not until 1785, after his return to London, that he began devoting himself primarily to painting the popular genre pictures for which he is best known today. Wheatley became a Royal Academician in 1791. He was attacked by gout, which eventually crippled him.

COUNTESS OF WARWICK AND HER CHILDREN

By George Romney (1734-1802) British School

The Frick Collection, New York
Canvas 78¼ x 60⅛ inches. Painted 1787-1788.

HENRIETTA, daughter of Richard Vernon of Hilton Park, Stafford, became the Countess of Warwick in 1776 upon her marriage to George Greville, second Earl of Warwick. The children in the painting are believed to be her daughter, Elizabeth, and her eldest son, Richard Henry.

The Countess, seated on a red brocaded armchair, wears a long-sleeved white satin gown with a white kerchief at her throat. In her powdered light brown hair, carefully curled and arranged around her beautiful face, she wears a bit of blue ribbon to match her eyes. Her right arm embraces her young daughter who leans against her. The girl's fingers touch her mother's hands. Elizabeth wears a white cap on the back of her blond hair. She has blue eyes and rosy cheeks. The broad sash of her low-cut white frock and the bows of her buff-colored slippers are both blue. Richard Henry appears uninterested in his mother and sister as he stands relaxed, his thumb tucked into his pocket and a hoop at his side. His blue coat, trimmed with silver buttons and a white frilled linen collar, fits over a buff-colored waistcoat and fawn-colored ankle-length trousers. White socks and black shoes with buckles complete his costume. His light-brown hair is dressed in the style of the period. In the background are distant hills, an expanse of cloud-filled sky and folds of heavy red drapery.

George Romney was born at Dalton-in-Furness, England. At the age of ten he began working for his father, a cabinetmaker. Young Romney occupied his leisure time carving wood figures, playing a violin he had made himself, and sketching the workmen in his father's shop. Impressed by the boy's talent for drawing, the elder Romney apprenticed his son at the age of nineteen to a little-known painter at Kendal in Westmorland County. In 1756 Romney married the daughter of his landlady, who had nursed him through a serious illness. After practicing six years as an itinerant painter in the northern counties of England, Romney left his wife and son—whom he saw only occasionally during the next thirty-seven years—to seek his fortune in London. Here his abilities were soon recognized. In 1773 Romney journeyed to Italy to study the Old Masters. Upon his return two years later he settled in London and soon had a practice that made him the rival of Sir Joshua Reynolds. Romney remained a successful painter in London until 1799, when failing health caused him to retire to Kendal, where his wife, whom he had neglected for so many years, cared for him.

MOTHER AND SON

By Thomas Sully (1783-1872) American School

The Metropolitan Museum of Art, New York
Canvas 57 x 45⅜ inches. Painted 1840.

THE BOY in this study, *Mother and Son,* is Francis Thomas Sully Darley, the grandson of the artist. The same boy bequeathed the painting to the Metropolitan Museum of Art in 1914.

Young Francis rests his curly blond head on his mother's shoulder. With one hand on her knee, he presses the other against the white glove of her left hand. His long dark-green buttoned coat has a white frill at the neck and his gray trousers touch the tops of his red shoes. The brown and white spaniel at the boy's feet looks up at his master's sensitive face. The mother sits pensively beside a low stone wall by the sea. She supports her head in her right hand as she leans on a carefully folded red-bordered shawl. Mrs. Darley's brown hair is looped up at the back with front curls falling forward over her delicate pink cheeks. Above her long white satin skirt is a brown bodice with white cuffs. A matching collar is trimmed with a blue bow. Towering in the background is a classical urn against a gray-blue sky.

Born in England, Thomas Sully was brought to America by his family when he was nine years old. His parents, who were actors, settled in Charleston, South Carolina, where the theater was an established part of the community. Sully first studied art with his brother-in-law, Jean Belzons, and his own brother Lawrence, both of whom were miniaturists. He worked later under John Trumbull and John Wesley Jarvis in New York and Gilbert Stuart in Boston. In 1809, the same year that Sully became an American citizen, he went to England to further his study. Several patrons helped to finance his trip, and to repay them Sully copied many of the paintings in Benjamin West's collection of Old Masters. It is said that he received some instruction from Benjamin West. However, the greatest single influence on Sully's style was the work of Sir Thomas Lawrence. Sully has often been called the "Sir Thomas Lawrence of America." Returning to Philadelphia the following year, 1810, he began some of his finest portraits. Sully was an industrious and popular painter. In addition to many hundreds of portraits, he also painted historical compositions, subject pictures and landscapes. Sully, who died on November 5, 1872, in his ninetieth year, was one of the few American artists of his time to leave a registry of his work.

22

Mrs. William Moseley and Her Son Charles

By Ralph Earl (1751-1801) American School

Yale University Art Gallery, New Haven
Canvas 86¾ x 68¼ inches. Painted 1791.

Laura Wolcott Moseley was the daughter of Oliver Wolcott, a signer of the Declaration of Independence and one-time Governor of Connecticut. Charles, her young son, was an only child. After graduating from Yale College, Charles practiced law until he died at the early age of twenty-eight.

On top of her dark brown, puffed hair, Mrs. Moseley wears a striking high-crowned white hat, trimmed with white plumes and hanging ornaments. An exaggerated hairdress emphasizes her sedate features. Her dark-blue, full-length coat, decorated with gold braid and brass buttons, is designed to reveal a frothy white jabot and a bit of the white skirt of the dress beneath. In her left hand she carries a pair of black gloves. With her right, she stays her restless son. Charles's blond curls are looped back over his ears. Deep bangs shorten the height of his forehead. His white ruffled collar, white socks, and black slippers, bring out the bright red color of his suit. Although both mother and son have fair complexions, their eyes are different; Mrs. Moseley's are blue, Charles's gray. The rich quality of their clothes indicates a family of good circumstance.

It was Ralph Earl's custom to paint his sitters in surroundings familiar to them. Here the background is a beautiful Connecticut landscape, with distant spires, rolling wooded hills, and meadows divided by a winding stream. The pale pink on the horizon and the blue-gray colors over the hills lend distance and space to the scene.

Ralph Earl, first-born son of Ralph and Phoebe Whittemore Earl, was born in Worcester County, Massachusetts, May 11, 1751. Little is known of his early life and training. In 1774 he settled in Connecticut to paint. The following year, he visited Lexington and Concord to sketch the first battle sites of the Revolutionary War. His sketches, engraved by his friend Amos Doolittle of New Haven, were the first American historical pictures. In 1779 Earl was in England painting portraits. In London he studied with Benjamin West. During the years 1783-1785, he exhibited at the Royal Academy. In the late eighties, he was back in America, working as an itinerant portrait painter, mostly in Connecticut, where he gained the patronage of many well-known families. Earl died at Bolton, Connecticut, on August 16, 1801.

MRS. AARON LOPEZ AND HER SON JOSHUA

By Gilbert Stuart (1755-1828) American School

The Detroit Institute of Arts, Detroit
Canvas 26 x 21½ inches. Painted c. 1772-1773.

MRS. LOPEZ, born Sarah Rivera, was the wife of one of the great merchants who made Newport, Rhode Island, an important harbor and trading center in the eighteenth century. Joshua, one of their ten children, later married the only daughter of the Reverend Isaac Touro, Newport's famous first Jewish minister. The portrait is one of Gilbert Stuart's earliest known works.

Dignified Mrs. López, is posed in a red chair against a neutral gray-blue background. On her thick black hair, worn in a pompadour to show her high forehead, is a white lace cap secured by a blue jeweled pin. Mrs. López' face is a lovely oval; her mouth is slightly smiling beneath a pert little nose. She has large brown almond-shaped eyes and a warm olive complexion. Her gray-blue silk gown with a softly draped collar has a fine white lace guimpe. A strand of pearls is entwined in the folds of the dress and pearl fastenings ornament its bodice. Young Joshua, about five or six years old, stands shoulder-high next to his mother. His brown hair is combed in the current fashion, back from the forehead and curled in rolls over the ears. Smartly dressed in a white suit and black bow tie, the boy closely resembles his handsome mother.

Gilbert Stuart, born near Narragansett Pier, Rhode Island, began his schooling at Newport. At fourteen he was painting portraits. A visiting Scots artist, Cosomo Alexander, attracted by the boy's talent, not only instructed him, but in 1772 took Stuart with him to Scotland. Unfortunately, Alexander died. Young Stuart was compelled to work his way back to Newport, where, about 1773, he set himself up as a portrait painter. However, two years later, Stuart returned to London. Here he had a difficult time until Benjamin West took him into his home and allowed him to work in his studio. Eventually Stuart met with success in London, but lived beyond his means. To escape the chance of debtors prison, he went to Ireland but suffered the same experience. With the hope of regaining his fortune and of satisfying a desire to paint President George Washington, Stuart returned to America in 1793. He first settled in New York and then moved to Philadelphia. In 1800, he went to live in the new city of Washington. But two years later, in 1805, he moved to Boston, where he continued his brilliant career until he died on July 9, 1828.

Mrs. John Nicholson and Son

By Charles Willson Peale (1741-1827) American School

Gift of Mr. and Mrs. Carter H. Harrison. The Art Institute of Chicago
Canvas 36 x 27⁵⁄₁₆ inches. Painted 1790.

Mrs. Nicholson was the wife of a Philadelphia financier who brought order to Pennsylvania's financial affairs after the Revolution. Nicholson was one of the wealthiest men of his day.

Mrs. Nicholson is posed against a dark-blue sky which shades to a rosy pink at the horizon. Rusty-brown and golden-yellow trees can be seen in the background. The little boy, in a dress of a thin, blue-white material, holds a sprig of light-yellow flowers in one hand and gently caresses his mother with the other. The large hat, worn at a jaunty angle over an egg-shell colored lace skull cap, is made of a light shiny blue silk and has a border of gold along its brim. Black and white feathers, caught up with blue ribbons, give it a dressy look. The boy's very fair, pink complexion and golden-brown eyebrows set off his wide-open blue eyes. Mrs. Nicholson's youthful beauty is enhanced by her soft, curly black hair. Her blue eyes gaze softly from a delicate, fair face. Her grayish-blue silk gown has a fichu and cuffs of the same color, made of a sheer material and ornamented with pearls. Around her waist is a stiff dark-blue sash, striped with tiny yellow dots.

Charles Willson Peale was born in Queen Anne's County, Maryland. He was apprenticed to a saddler after the early death of his schoolmaster father, but in young manhood turned from saddlery to portrait painting. John Hesselius and John Singleton Copley helped and advised him, and friends at Annapolis sent him to London for two years' study with Benjamin West. The Revolutionary War took him to Philadelphia, where he served as an officer in Washington's army and as a representative in the General Assembly. He sketched many of the American military figures that became part of the exhibition gallery of portraits he set up adjoining his Philadelphia studio. Later, in 1786, he added a museum of natural history to his gallery, the first scientific museum in America. In 1805 Peale became one of the founders of the Pennsylvania Academy of the Fine Arts at Philadelphia.

Charles Willson Peale was the head of a notable family of artists. He taught painting to his children and his brother, James. On February 22, 1827, Charles Willson Peale, artist, patriot and naturalist, died in Philadelphia.

Mrs. Benjamin West and Her Son Raphael

By Benjamin West (1738-1820) American School

The Charles W. Harkness Gift. The Cleveland Museum of Art
Canvas 26¼ x 26 inches. Painted 1770.

Benjamin West married Elizabeth Shewell some months after his arrival in England in 1763. Elizabeth, an orphan, lived with her brother in Philadelphia. The brother was opposed to her marriage to West; in fact, he held her captive in her room so that she could not go to him. Friends of the artist, including Benjamin Franklin, plotted and successfully carried out a midnight escape and a voyage to England for her. Raphael was their first-born child.

The mother and child are painted against a background that suggests a dark, red-brown tree trunk, blue-green foliage and a bit of blue sky. Gracefully draped over the mother's head and caught at the back of her neck is a plum-colored scarf edged with gold fringe. The scarf forms a mantle over her shoulders that meets the soft green, gold embroidered shawl drawn over her arm. Fine brown hair, soft brown eyes, and straight, well-formed brows accent her pale coloring and her classical features. Her mouth is curved in a smile. Young Raphael, in a flowing white robe, supports himself by resting an arm on his mother's shoulder. His reddish, light-brown hair falls in uneven strands about his round face. His blue eyes look straight ahead as he presses a delicately flushed cheek against his mother.

Benjamin West, the first American artist to win international fame, was born in what is now Swarthmore, Pennsylvania. By the age of eleven he was painting landscapes and shortly thereafter received commissions for portraits. A Cherokee Indian chief is said to have taught him to mix colors. West studied painting in Philadelphia under William Williams. In 1760, he set out for Italy to study. Three years later he moved to England, where he spent the rest of his life. He opened a studio in London and became famous for his large historical works. In 1772 West, who had assisted in the founding of the Royal Academy, became historical painter to George III. Upon the death of Sir Joshua Reynolds in 1792, West was made the second president of the Royal Academy. Three generations of American artists flocked to his studio for guidance and instruction. Among them were Charles Willson Peale and his son, Rembrandt, Washington Allston, John Trumbull, Thomas Sully, Gilbert Stuart, Robert Fulton and Samuel F. B. Morse. West died in London and was buried in St. Paul's Cathedral.

INFANTA MARIA LUISA AND HER SON CARLOS LUIS

By Francisco de Goya (1746-1828) Spanish School

The Metropolitan Museum of Art, New York
Canvas 39⅛ x 27 inches. Painted 1800.

THE INFANTA Maria Luisa, Princess of Parma, was the daughter of Charles IV and his queen, Maria Luisa of Spain.

The Infanta, about eighteen years old, is posed with her baby son before a dark gray-blue and brown background. Thick reddish-brown, curled hair, studded with diamonds, crowns her small head and face. Elegantly curved, light brown brows complement her large, brown-flecked black eyes. The diamonds of her elaborate pendant earrings and double strand necklace gleam blue-white against the deep flesh tones of her skin. Shades of copper brown are reflected in the sheer, gray-white silk of the Infanta's high-waisted gown. Across her bodice is the blue and white band of the Order of Maria Luisa; the gold medallion hangs from a black velvet ribbon pinned to the dress. On her left arm is a gold bracelet worn over a transparent gray-white glove. Carlos Luis also wears the Order of Maria Luisa. His long dress is the same gray-white as his mother's. The ties of his blue-gray cap go under his fat little chin and end in a bow at the top of his head. Wisps of blond hair fringe the forehead of his pink face, with its gray eyes.

Francisco de Goya was born in a small town near Saragossa in Spain. Early he gave evidence of an artistic ability and at the age of fourteen was apprenticed to a painter in Saragossa. Apparently he was a reckless youth, for a series of escapades caused him to move often. He studied in Madrid under Francisco Bayeu, a painter at the court. Then followed a year in Rome. By 1775 Goya seems to have settled down. He was back in Madrid and married to Josefa Bayeu, the sister of his former teacher. Shortly after, he received a royal commission to design a tapestry, the first of a famous series he was to execute. From that time on he received many honors and in 1799 was made First Court Painter to Charles IV. Between 1808 and 1812, Goya served the court of the French conquerors of Spain. It was during this period that Goya made a long series of etchings that showed his hatred of war. In 1824 he went to Bordeaux, France, for his health. Here he continued to paint and etch, and to experiment with the new technique of lithography. At this time a friend said that he was "deaf, aged, awkward and weak . . . but is quite contented and wants to see people." Goya was still active and concerned with human affairs when he died in Bordeaux.

MADAME GUILLON-LETHIERE AND HER SON

By Jean Auguste Dominique Ingres (1780-1867) French School

The Metropolitan Museum of Art, New York
Pencil on white paper 11¹³⁄₁₆ x 8¾ inches. Executed 1819.

MADAME GUILLON-LETHIERE was the daughter-in-law of Guillaume Guillon-Lethière, the painter and Director of the French Academy in Rome while Ingres studied there.

With great precision of line, Ingres has drawn this charming portrait of Madame Guillon-Lethière. She is seated in a low, straight-backed chair, her small son, Charles Paul Joachim Guillaume, at her side. Her daytime gown, with long sleeves and a frilled ruff, is of the Directoire period, its high waistline ornamented by a narrow sash. Madame Guillon-Lethière, following the classical influence of the time, has bound her hair with three bands of ribbon, allowing her short curls to fall forward. Arched eyebrows, over her large oval slanting eyes, accent her wide forehead and high cheekbones. The small mouth, with a full lower lip, is drawn upward in a curve, adding to her dreamy and pleasant expression. The young Charles, with deep-set eyes, small nose and mouth, appears alert and restive, but is quieted by his mother's restraining hands.

Jean Auguste Dominique Ingres was born on August 29, 1780, at Montauban in southern France. He received his first lessons in drawing and music from his father, who was a talented artist and musician. At eleven, he was enrolled in the Academy of Fine Arts at Toulouse. A copy of Raphael's *Madonna of the Chair* which he saw there affected his art for the rest of his life. Coming to Paris in 1797, he entered the studio of Jacques Louis David, then the acknowledged leader of French art. In 1801 the young Ingres won the Prix de Rome, an award for study in Italy, but lack of national funds delayed his journey until 1806. Meanwhile, he became an accomplished artist. When Ingres finally reached Italy he remained eighteen years, fourteen in Rome, four in Florence. After the fall of Napoleon, he helped earn his living by drawing many pencil portraits. Finally, he was awarded a commission by his own government to paint *The Vow of Louis XIII* for the cathedral of his native Montauban. When exhibited in the Paris Salon of 1824, the picture made him famous almost overnight. The rest of his long and successful career was passed in Rome and Paris.

MOTHER AND CHILD ON BEACH

By Jean Baptiste Camille Corot (1796-1875) French School

John G. Johnson Collection, Philadelphia
Canvas 14⅞ x 18⅛ inches. Painted 1860-1870.

I HAVE only one goal in life, which I desire to pursue with constancy: that is to paint landscapes," Jean Baptiste Camille Corot is recorded as saying. Aside from achieving his ambition with hundreds of beautiful landscapes, Corot produced many notable figure studies. *Mother and Child on Beach* is among them. The picture was painted sometime during the last fifteen years of Corot's life. It now hangs in the Philadelphia Museum of Art.

The mother kneels on a white blanket and stretches out her arms to make the little one comfortable. Strands of dark hair, showing beneath a white cap, frame the little girl's round face. She wears a long mauve-colored dress. Black shoes partially cover her coarse blue stockings. Over a white blouse and above a full amber-brown skirt, the mother wears a black bodice. To brighten the costume she has bound her black hair with a red ribbon. Her dark eyes are set under heavy brows in a swarthy face. The sea and the sky merge in silvery tones of gray. Receding dark cliffs and a sailboat on the horizon create a feeling of distance and space.

Jean Baptiste Camille Corot was the son of a successful Parisian milliner. After finishing school at Rouen, he was apprenticed for three years to a linen draper, but spent his spare time in drawing and painting. In 1822, when Corot was twenty-six, his father finally consented to his taking up art as a career. He studied first under Achille Michallon, then under Jean Victor Bertin. The latter stimulated Corot's interest in classical art and taught him that Italy was the goal of all artists. The generous allowance given by his father enabled Corot to make the first of three trips to Italy in 1825. He stayed for three years, painting in Rome and other parts of Italy, until his return to France. The paintings of that first stay in Italy are among Corot's most prized works. He first exhibited at the Paris Salon in 1827 and was a regular exhibitor thereafter. By the early 1840's he had won acclaim as a landscapist. In 1846 he was decorated with the Legion of Honor. Never lacking for funds, Corot generously helped others. In addition to several hundred landscapes and numerous figure studies, Corot executed etchings, decorated panels for friends' homes, and painted decorations for churches. Corot's serene personality is reflected in his work.

Fisherman's Wife and Child

By Théodore Chassériau (1819-1856) French School

Museum of Art, Rhode Island School of Design, Providence
Panel-Wood 6¾₆ x 5¼₆ inches. Date unknown.

THIS idealized mother and child was exhibited at the Paris Salon of 1851. At the time it was described as "pure and noble as an antique cameo."

The fisherman's wife and her child sit on a rock, which juts out from the edge of a greenish-blue sea. Painted in somber tones, the figures are dramatically posed against a medium blue sky, brilliant with strokes of pink and white. Behind the rock on the right appears to be a sailing craft. The mother wears a white cap over her light brown hair. The short left sleeve of her brownish dress reveals the edge of an undergarment, painted in white, orange-yellow and dull blue. Her long skirt, tucked up behind her leg, exposes a bare foot, resting firmly on the rock. Tender and possessive, the mother supports her blond-haired child in an upright position. The baby fondles her with its right hand and kisses her bronzed cheek. Its tanned body is partially covered by a white sheet, cast with pink.

Théodore Chassériau was born on the island of Santo Domingo. He was the son of the French Secretary-General of the island. At the age of three he was taken to France. He was scarcely more than twelve when he became a pupil of Ingres. At seventeen he was awarded a medal of the third class at the Paris Salon. Three years later, Chassériau's *Susanna and the Elders* and *Venus Anadyomene* brought him wide acclaim. The next year he rejoined Ingres, then Director of the French Academy in Rome. Although his master's style showed in his numerous portraits, Chassériau's other themes were painted with more emotion. When Chassériau visited Algeria in 1846, the color and movement of Arab lands confirmed his new manner. Thereafter, his desert warriors, his scenes from Shakespeare and mythology all show a freer style. Returning to Paris, he completed his most famous work, the stairway of the Cour des Comptes, now largely destroyed, in the Palais d'Orsay. Later he designed murals for the churches of Saint-Roch and Saint-Philippe-du-Roule. At thirty he was made a Chevalier of the Legion of Honor. Seven years later, on October 8, 1856, his brilliant career was suddenly ended by a fatal illness.

MOTHER AND CHILDREN

By Albert Neuhuijs (1844-1914) Dutch School

Gift of Edward Drummond Libbey. The Toledo Museum of Art
Oil on oak 12⅝ x 9¼ inches. Date unknown.

IN THIS appealing Dutch interior, the mother attending the little one on her lap sits before a crudely made table of reddish-brown wood. A yellow-green basin has been placed on the table. Dressed in white, the reddish-haired baby lies comfortable and contented on a white blanket. The sallow-faced mother smiles as she fastens a pin to the baby's garment. She wears a gray wool skirt, a brown jacket and a cap over her dark-brown hair. Standing at the mother's elbow, with a slice of bread in its hand, the blond-haired child watches the mother and baby. The child's light-blue dress and white cotton pinafore hang to the top of its wooden shoes.

Albert Neuhuijs was born in Utrecht. He became a pupil of G. Graevanger and of the Antwerp Academy. He began his career by painting historical subjects and portraits, but in 1870, he turned to painting the humble scenes of everyday life that have become a tradition in Dutch art. He took particular delight in describing the domestic life of mothers with their children. Neuhuijs participated in many international exhibitions, receiving high recognition. His works are to be found in museums throughout the Western World, the largest collection being in Amsterdam. Neuhuijs died at Locarno on February 6, 1914.

THE STOCKING

By Mary Cassatt (1845-1926) American School

Lucas Collection on Permanent Loan to the Baltimore Museum of Art
Drypoint 10¼ x 7⁵⁄₁₆ inches. Executed in 1890.

I WILL not admit a woman can draw like that!" exclaimed the French artist, Edgar Degas, upon seeing a work by Mary Cassatt. She was indeed an excellent draftsman.

Mary Cassatt, as she has done in *The Stocking*, often interpreted the tenderness of a mother's love. This work was the third in a series of twelve drypoint etchings exhibited in Paris in 1891. The seated mother, serene and confident, is shown dressing her little one. Her broad features are softened by the simple arrangement of her hair. The playful child, comfortable and secure on her mother's ample lap, turns her neatly brushed head to the side. She reaches out a chubby hand toward something.

Mary Cassatt was born in Pittsburgh, Pennsylvania. Her father was a banker, her mother an exceptionally well-educated woman. Between the ages of five and ten Mary Cassatt lived in France. Upon returning to America, her family settled in Philadelphia. Here at the Pennsylvania Academy of the Fine Arts, Mary Cassatt studied cast drawing. At twenty-three, despite her family's disapproval, she sailed for Europe to further her study of art. After copying the Old Masters in Italy, Spain, Belgium, and Holland, she settled in Paris in 1874. Her paintings were shown there at the Salon during three consecutive years, but in 1877 her entry was refused. At this point the artist, Edgar Degas, who had never met her but was impressed by her talent, asked her to exhibit with the Impressionist group. "I accepted with joy," she told her biographer. "Now I could work with absolute independence without considering the opinion of a jury. I had already recognized who were my true masters. I admired Manet, Courbet, and Degas. I took leave of conventional art—I began to live." But such living was trying, since in those days the Impressionists were scoffed at. It was not until the first exhibition of her work in Paris in 1891 that Mary Cassatt's reputation became fully established.

MOTHER AND CHILDREN

By Pierre Auguste Renoir (1841-1919) French School

The Frick Collection, New York
Canvas 66⅛ x 41¼ inches. Painted 1874.

IT IS not definitely known who the mother and the children are in this picture. It is believed that Renoir painted them while he was living in Paris.

The young mother gently guides her two daughters along the sandy path of a public garden. Her bonnet, trimmed with rosebuds, blue lace and white ruching, sits high on her light-brown hair. Brown eyes look out from her young face with its shell-pearl coloring and well-shaped mouth. She wears a violet-gray dress with white collar and cuffs and a blue bow. A sapphire-blue jacket, trimmed with brown fur, and white gloves complete her outfit. Her brown-eyed, rosy-cheeked daughters are dressed alike. Perched on their long, wavy golden hair are white caps, fur-trimmed, with small blue velvet crowns. Their blue-green coats, worn over matching frocks, are edged with white fur. Both children wear white gaiters and white shoes. The older child clasps her precious blue-eyed doll, dressed in a dark jacket, pink skirt and white crinoline. The doll's hair is the same color as that of her owner's. The younger girl, with an air of satisfaction, warms her hands in her muff. In the right background at the edge of a lavender flower bed, a group tarries on the park walk. Their costumes range from light blue to medium gray-blue, with touches of black and white. Patiently waiting on the path to continue their outing are two dogs. High shrubbery in varying shades of green with brown-mauve shadows border the opposite side.

Pierre Auguste Renoir, born at Limoges, France, was the son of a tailor. In his early years young Renoir worked in a china factory, painting delicate figures and floral patterns on porcelain. Later he found employment in decorating fans with copies of the paintings of Watteau, Boucher and Fragonard. When he had saved enough money, Renoir entered Gleyre's studio in Paris, where he began seriously to study painting. By the time he reached his late sixties, his hands had become so crippled that he could no longer hold a brush. But Renoir was not to be denied the work that was life itself to him. With brushes strapped to his hands, he continued to paint pictures that still achieved that beauty and joy which Renoir felt were essential to art.

MADAME BOURSIER AND DAUGHTER

By Berthe Morisot (1841-1895) French School

The Brooklyn Museum, Brooklyn, New York
Canvas 29½ x 22½ inches. Painted 1876.

BERTHE MORISOT'S sitters were usually people of her own class—often members of her own family. She painted them, as she has painted her cousins, *Madame Boursier and Daughter,* in the pleasant and comfortable surroundings of the well-to-do French middle class.

As if she were paying a call, Madame Boursier, with her small daughter, is shown in a mid-nineteenth-century parlor. She sits composed, her gray eyes fixed in polite attention. Her delicate pink complexion and soft curling brown hair are set off by a black jacket, painted with purple undertones in its folds. The coat she wears has wide lapels and a stand-up collar. A small pink rose and a white frill ornament its neckline. A feathered, black hat sits high on her head. The only jewelry Madame Boursier wears are pendant earrings. She sits in a chair which has been covered in a white fabric printed with a design of twining red flowers. Her young daughter sits quietly beside her. The reddish-orange bow on the little girl's medium-blond hair accents the gray of her eyes and heightens the red of her cheeks. Her high-collared, white blouse is worn under a light blue-gray jacket trimmed in white. The colors of the background vary from gray to brownish yellow and a lighter ocher. On top of the piano is a white vase with a blue pattern.

Berthe Morisot was born in Bourges, France. Her father was originally trained as an architect but later became a Paris magistrate. After her first lessons with Chocarne, a painter of little note, she studied under Joseph Guichard, a pupil of both Ingres and Delacroix. Her insistent desire to paint out-of-doors, however, led her to Corot, who became her friend and guide. In 1868 she met Edouard Manet. A firm friendship developed between the two artists. The Manet and Morisot families saw much of each other and in 1874 Berthe married the painter's brother, Eugène, but still signed her work "Berthe Morisot." That same year she began exhibiting with the Impressionists at their initial show. She spent many of her holidays traveling on the Continent, studying the works of the Old Masters. A critic has said of Berthe Morisot, "All her work is bathed in brightness, in azure, in sunlight: it is a woman's work, but it has strength, a freedom of touch and an originality which one would hardly have expected."

PORTRAIT OF A BOY

By John Singer Sargent (1856-1925) American School

Collection of Carnegie Institute, Pittsburgh
Canvas 56 x 40 inches. Painted 1890.

HOMER SAINT-GAUDENS, the young boy in the portrait, was of an illustrious family. His father was the American sculptor, Augustus Saint-Gaudens, and his mother was a cousin of the artist, Winslow Homer.

In this picture, ten-year-old Homer sits on a brown, carved-oak chair, apparently resigned to, though somewhat bored by, having his portrait painted. His mother reads to him from one of his favorite books, *Blue Jackets of '76*. His dark, gray-blue suit, with knee breeches, has a flowing white tie which falls over the top of a high-buttoned vest. His shiny patent-leather shoes are in sharp contrast to his long, dull-black ribbed stockings. The boy's brown hair, worn over the forehead, emphasizes his large, wide-spaced dark eyes and handsome face. The angle of Mrs. Saint-Gaudens' head shows her black hair, knotted and held in place by a black comb. Her eyes, set in an oval face, are lowered, and her lips parted, as she reads. A black velvet band and a red rose decorate her gray blouse, which she wears over a full, light gray skirt. A multicolored rug in the foreground merges into the blacks and dark browns of the background.

John Singer Sargent was born in Florence, Italy, of American parents. His mother encouraged her son's talents. His notebooks show that from the age of thirteen, wherever the family traveled, he was busily recording scenery and people. At eighteen, Sargent entered the studio of Carolus Duran, in Paris. He paid his first visit to the United States when he was twenty. It was in the following year, 1877, that he sent his first picture, *The Portrait of Miss Watts,* to the Paris Salon. In 1879 and 1880, Sargent went to Spain and Holland. In Spain he studied the works of Velasquez; in Holland, those of Frans Hals. Both of these trips were of great importance to his later work. He exhibited regularly at the Paris Salon until the furor of protest raised against his full-length portrait of Madame Gautreau, now in New York's Metropolitan Museum of Art, in 1884. After this, Sargent moved to London, where he lived permanently. During frequent trips to America he was welcomed with enthusiasm. He painted many prominent Americans and also murals for Boston's Public Library and Museum of Fine Arts. Sargent in later years spent more and more time in Switzerland and the south of Europe, where he painted water colors, which he preferred to portraits.

EMMA AND HER CHILDREN

By George Bellows (1882-1925) American School

Museum of Fine Arts, Boston
Canvas 59 x 65 inches. Painted 1923.

FROM 1920 through 1924 George Bellows spent his summers in Woodstock, New York. There he painted his wife, Emma, and their two daughters, Anne, twelve, and Jean, eight.

The family is shown in full light against a somber putty-colored background. Dark red curtains frame the windows. Emma sits at one end of a black, horsehair sofa, with Jean on her knees. She wears a striped black gown, made of sheer silk material, with a long black sash falling to the floor. A turned-up collar, lined in frilled white organdie, is held in place by a black, heirloom brooch. Emma's brown hair is piled high at the back of her head with bangs over her forehead. Black earrings accent her blue eyes and delicate coloring. She holds a folding, painted fan in her right hand. In striking contrast to her mother's dark gown, Jean wears a white, dotted-swiss dress, cut with a full skirt. Her gray-blue eyes, set wide apart, look intently across the room. Her oval face is framed by long bangs and shoulder-length, straight golden hair. Anne, at the other end of the sofa, appears preoccupied. Her long bangs and wavy blond hair emphasize her lovely face. A fringed shawl of a pale gray-green color partially hides her soft, red-checkered voile dress. When the painting was finished, Jean and Anne each received the well-earned, ten-dollar bills promised them by their father.

George Bellows was born in Columbus, Ohio. He was the son of an architect and builder and the grandson of a whaling captain. In 1904 he left Ohio State University to study at the New York School of Art under Robert Henri. His career as a recognized artist really began when he received the second Hallagarten prize at the National Academy in 1908. The following year he sold his first painting and was elected an Associate Member of the Academy of Design, the youngest man to be so honored. Bellows married Emma Louise Story in 1910. Their children, Anne and Jean, were often the subject of his pictures. Bellows painted sporting events, portraits of his family and friends, landscapes and scenes of interest to him. In addition to his painting, he was adept at drawing and lithography. Bellows died at the height of his career, January 8, 1925, at the age of forty-two. In 1957 the National Gallery of Art in Washington held as its first one-man exhibition a comprehensive showing of the art of George Bellows.

Mother and Child

By Gari Melchers (1860-1932) American School

Gift of James Deering. The Art Institute of Chicago
Canvas 25 x 21⅜ inches. Painted c. 1906.

Gari Melchers lived for many years in the provinces of France and Holland and came to know the sturdy wholesome people he portrayed. The mother and child was one of his favorite themes. This version probably shows a neighboring family.

The cheerful baby, in a clean white dress, radiates health and contentment. Securely held in the mother's arms and wrapped in a mauve-colored shawl, it turns its blond head toward the artist. Its blue eyes look out from above plump, rosy cheeks. The small mouth is slightly opened. The baby's chubby hands, playfully touch the mother. The woman's simply combed, reddish-brown hair is drawn back over her ears. She has high cheekbones and a firm chin. The dark skin of her broad face harmonizes with the browns of her coarse garment. The straightforward look in the mother's green eyes shows an inner peace as she holds her child.

Whether he painted a portrait or included his sitters as part of a landscape, Gari Melchers lived up to the motto he had hung over the door of his studio, "Waar en Klaar" (True and Clear).

The son of a sculptor, woodcarver and decorator, Gari Melchers was born in Detroit, Michigan. At seventeen he was sent by his parents to study at the Royal Academy at Düsseldorf. Four years later, in 1881, he was in Paris at the Ecole des Beaux Arts. When he was but twenty-two, Melchers exhibited at the Salon. After six years away from home, Melchers visited America in 1884. Returning to Paris the following year, he opened a studio there and another at Egmond in Holland. He divided his time between these two places and also made frequent trips to America. Many of his visits to this country were devoted to portraiture and mural painting. Two of his murals are in the Library of Congress. In 1909, Melchers accepted the invitation of the Grand Duke of Saxe-Weimar to teach at Weimar, where he was given a large pavilion with studios. His art covered many subjects. He was honored in his own country and Europe with such awards as the Legion of Honor of France and membership in the American Academy of Arts and Letters. With the outbreak of World War I he and his wife, the former Corinne Lawton Mackall of Savannah, Georgia, took up permanent residence in Virginia.

THE LITTLE MADONNA

By George Benjamin Luks (1867-1933) American School

Addison Gallery of American Art, Phillips Academy, Andover, Massachusetts
Canvas 27 x 22 inches. Painted 1905.

GEORGE LUKS found many of his subjects in the poor sections of New York. *The Little Madonna,* as he called this work, expresses the universal love of a little girl for her doll-child.

The little mother sits on a reddish-brown curbstone before a dark-red wall clasping her child possessively. Having placed the doll's arms about her neck, she gazes into its face, pressing her lips against its china cheek. The little girl's wispy red hair outshines the white bow obscured by shadows at the back of her head. An oversized creamy-white dress falls in wrinkled folds over her short legs. The long blond curls of the large doll hang down over its dark gray-blue dress. High dark boots reach nearly to its knees. In the background a dark bluish-gray figure watches from the doorway of a gray-green building. The painting with its creamy whites and russet tones has the color of a mellow autumn.

George Luks was born in Williamsport, Pennsylvania, where he lived until he entered the Pennsylvania Academy of the Fine Arts in Philadelphia. Later he studied in Germany, Paris and London. When he returned to America he worked as an illustrator and correspondent for the *Philadelphia Bulletin.* In the last part of the century he settled in New York as staff artist and cartoonist for the *New York World* until the early 1900's, when he turned to painting city life. Luks was an amateur prize fighter in his youth, and painted several canvases of the ring, but most of his work was devoted to the people of the streets of New York. He was an influential teacher, first at the Art Students League of New York and later at his own school.

Quaker Mother and Child

By Horace Pippin (1888-1946) American School

Rhode Island School of Design, Providence
Canvas 15 x 20 inches. Painted 1944 (?)

HORACE PIPPIN painted as he was inspired. "Pictures just come to my mind," he said, "and I tell my heart to go ahead."

In this canvas of an early Quaker interior, the mother, in a white bonnet, with a black-fringed shawl draped over her gray dress, sits in a hard straight-backed chair. She pauses from her work on a red, white and green quilt to look at the needle in her hand. Beside her, in a crude wooden cradle, painted gray-brown, her black-haired child sleeps contentedly under a grayish-white blanket. A flaming red fire helps to brighten the bleak room with its light-gray walls. Small white-fringed rugs with red, black and white stripes are scattered over the gray-brown, wide-board floors. Balancing the grandfather's clock is a small mullioned window. Iron cooking utensils hang from the wall between the window and fireplace, and large pots and pans sit on the floor beneath. Ready for use, in a handy place on the mantel, is a white candle in its holder, and over it a brown and black gun with a natural-colored bone powder horn.

Horace Pippin was born in West Chester, Pennsylvania. He was interested in art even as a child. During his spelling lessons in elementary school in Goshen, New York, where he had moved with his mother, he sketched beside his words the objects for which they stood. At the age of ten Pippin crayoned and painted water color pictures of Biblical subjects on muslin squares, fraying the edges so as to make them look like doilies. These were sold at a Sunday school festival. When he was fourteen, his employer, whose portrait he had drawn, offered to send him to art school. His mother's illness prevented this, but Pippin never lost his interest in art. After working in a coal yard, a feed store, a hotel, a storage house, and a brakehouse company, Pippin enlisted in the army in 1917. He was badly wounded in World War I and was honorably discharged in 1919. The following year he married and settled in West Chester. Despite his injured hand, he was able to carry on his painting, using his left hand to grip his right and steady his brush. In 1930 Pippin began painting his memories of the war. Seven years later, he was given an exhibition at the West Chester Community Center. Pippin's reputation as a primitive artist was well established before he died at West Chester on July 6, 1946.

PORTRAIT OF MOTHER AND CHILD

By an unknown artist. American School

The Newark Museum, Newark, New Jersey
Canvas 27 x23 inches. Date unknown.

THE mother and child in this portrait, as well as the artist who painted it, are unknown. It is not known whether the child is a boy or a girl.

Against a background of red and brown the mother is shown with her child on her lap. She embraces the child and supports it with her long-fingered hand. The brown color of the mother's dress, with its fringed shoulder cape, almost fades into the background of the picture, so that the white lingerie collar and white cap form a soft frame for her rather stern face. Pale-pink ribbon ties, fastened to the cap she wears at the back of her head, hang over her shoulders. Her braided, brown hair emphasizes her long oval face, with its brown eyes, long straight nose, and set mouth. The gold chain about her short, thickset neck falls over the front of her dress, and is caught up by the floral mosaic pin that fastens her collar. Her pendant earrings are set with large, cut stones. The child's blue frock, with a long skirt and shirred bodice, is edged at the neck and sleeves with narrow white lace. Fair hair, drawn back from a part in the center, lies flat on the head. The child's small mouth and alert blue eyes are about to break into a smile as it fingers the gold beads and clutches the black handle of a brass bell.

Like many other works of American folk art, the authorship of this portrait remains anonymous. During colonial days and ever since, there have been artists who have had no training but who have painted portraits, historical subjects, religious pictures and many other themes. These pictures, which often seem childlike, and so are called primitive, are decorative and charming. In recent years the interest in this form of American art has grown enormously.

Madame Roulin and Her Baby

By Vincent van Gogh (1853-1890) Dutch French School

Lisa Norris Elkins Collection, Philadelphia Museum of Art
Canvas 30½ x 29 inches. Painted 1888-1889.

Vincent van Gogh lived among the friendly, simple peasants at Arles in southern France during the latter part of his life. Among his friends in that village, he counted Roulin, a postman, as a favorite. On several occasions, members of the Roulin family posed for him.

Against a bright yellow background, suggestive of the sunshine of southern France, Madame Roulin sits in a reddish-brown arm chair, holding her baby. The woman's figure, clad in a grass-green dress, is strongly outlined in dark blue-greens. The hair is indicated by bold brush strokes of blue, green and yellow, with the repeated use of the dark outline. The planes and features of Madame Roulin's face are accented by reflections of an orange-red light. The baby is supported by the mother's strong hands. The same dark blue-greens are again used to outline the baby's close-fitting white cap and long dress with full sleeves. The attention of the little one's dark eyes appears to rest on something unseen, perhaps on the artist himself.

The son of a pastor and the nephew of three art dealers, Vincent van Gogh developed a passionate interest in both the Bible and art. He was born at Groot Zundert in the Dutch Branbant, March 30, 1853. As a young man he worked for the Goupil Art Gallery; first at The Hague, then at Brussels, London, and Paris. Later, he enrolled in a seminary at Brussels, but gave up his studies to become an evangelist, working among the miners in the poorest part of Belgium. Van Gogh lived in poverty and shared the sufferings of those he tried to help. His first important art efforts were studies of these people. Encouraged in art by his brother Theo, who worked for Goupil, he went to Paris in 1886 and there came under the influence of the Impressionists. Color became the dominant interest in his painting. In 1888, van Gogh left Paris for Arles in the south of France, where he did his most important work. He died at Auvers, July 29, 1890, at the age of thirty-seven.

Mother and Child

By Pablo Picasso (1881-   ) French School

Cone Collection, Baltimore Museum of Art
Canvas 39½ x 31½ inches. Painted 1922.

Pablo Picasso is an artist who has painted in many styles. This study of mother and child belongs to his "classic" period which began soon after World War I. At the time, Picasso's son, Paolo, was a very young child. He doubtless inspired his father to paint this picture.

The painting has the tender, delicate quality of a drawing. The figures are sketched with very few lines. Thin washes of color, grayish-green in the background, subtle tans and sepia on the figures, and a light blue for the boy's sweater, add warmth to the subject. The mother holds the child in her lap, supporting him with a strong hand. Her hair falls loosely over her shoulder. A hip-length jacket covers her simple dress. The boy amuses himself by pulling at what appears to be a kerchief held by the mother in her right hand. Over his suit he wears a sweater. In the background Picasso has sketched the graceful tracery of a leafy vine.

Pablo Ruíz Picasso, one of the most influential artists and dominant personalities of the twentieth century, was born at Malaga, Spain. His father, an art teacher, aware of his son's unusual talent, encouraged and instructed him. A large canvas by him, now in the Malaga Gallery, was painted, it is said, when Picasso was nine. When he was thirteen, his family settled in Barcelona. So gifted was he that he finished in one day the entrance requirements of the Academy, for which a month was allowed. In 1896 he exhibited a painting at the Barcelona biennial show. He was then fourteen. In 1897, in Madrid, he was admitted with the same distinction to the Royal Academy of San Fernando. But dissatisfied with the teaching he withdrew to Barcelona. Between 1900 and 1902 Picasso paid three visits to Paris, during which time he sold several paintings, studied the Louvre collections, the post-Impressionists, and exhibited in two art galleries. In 1904 he settled in Paris, returning intermittently to Spain and traveling on the Continent. Picasso has not only painted but has done book illustration, stage and costume design, etching and lithography, and sculpture. His interest in ceramics in recent years has taken much of his time. In 1957 the Museum of Modern Art, New York, honored Picasso's seventy-fifth anniversary by giving him one of the most comprehensive one-man shows ever assembled.